MW00324731

THE

LITTLE
BRIC
BOOK

Cracking the code

for global management

of projects in Brazil, Russia,

India and China.

THE

LITTLE

BRIC

BOOK

BRANDI MOORE

ISBN: 978-0-615-40899-6

Book cover and interior design by Susan Newman Design Inc.

Table of Contents

CHAPTER 1: INTRODUCTION

At the start of 2010, I was asked to talk about the BRIC at a large conference. While I have worked with the BRIC countries – Brazil, Russia, India and China – my primary focus is India. After extensive research, I was surprised to learn these four countries, at their core, have similar ways of doing business. Ways that are different from the United States. Understanding these differences is critical for Corporate America.

Broken down, the core principles of doing business are:
- How teams work together
- How employees view their relationship with their organization
- How organizations prefer to engage with partners
- How organizations communicate
- And how power is managed inside unequal systems in organizations

These principles make corporations tick inside and engage from the outside. The BRIC holds the same cultural business preferences across these five core principles that impact the underlying foundation of business relationships. Unfortunately these principles are different than American business preferences, making it critical for Americans to consider adapting approaches to develop strong partnerships. Without this knowledge, American workers are at a disadvantage. This disadvantage is growing at lightning speed as the BRIC sets out on its predicted 20-year path of economic success.

This book will help you navigate this tough period in the American workplace. The truth is that the American worker has been left behind. Organizations are so focused on profit margins that come from leveraging the BRIC countries they have forgotten it's the American worker who makes it happen. This worker is likely without a passport and has probably never left the US.

1.1 The Silent Change

President Barack Obama was inaugurated wearing a Hickey Freeman suit. Most Americans don't realize that Hickey Freeman is now owned by SKNL, an Indian firm based in Mumbai. Soon all of their clothing will be made in India. This American brand, now run by an Indian interest, continues to be advertised as an American icon.

This is just one example of how the world is changing – changing behind the scenes. Brands that used to be American are being bought up by the newly cash rich BRIC corporations. The speed of this change was sent into high gear as America entered a deep recession in 2008. No market vertical has been spared.

The American worker is feeling the change as they are increasingly engaged with the BRIC countries as American corporations scramble to find new paths for growth. At the 2010 Outsourcing World Summit held by the International Association of Outsourcing Professionals, Mahadeva Matt Mani, a partner at Booz & Company, delivered the closing speech on the complexity of global business. One of the things he said was that the world has not figured out how to develop global talent. He's right.

This book is about developing a specific kind of global talent: The Desk Diplomat. Each day, the Desk Diplomat is confronted with global interactions without the benefit of an expatriate experience. These vigilant workers are being left behind because American companies don't offer thorough training. More often, companies provide short courses on cross-cultural information that is meaningless to their daily challenge. I was educated through this process and found it unhelpful because these trainings are designed for expatriates, not those who continue to drive projects to fruition from their desk. These efforts let Corporate America off the hook: once you have been "trained" you are expected to understand.

1.2 The Goal of The Little BRIC Book

If you are preparing to engage in a business relationship with the BRIC, this book will help you get started. If you are already engaged with the BRIC, this book can help you excel at managing your project to completion. It is designed to offer insights into business cultures and inform you on how to develop business relationships. Most of us don't have time to become culture experts; we need answers on how to get projects moving to meet objectives. This book is designed to answer that call. You can use it to understand more about how these cultures are different from ours or as a reference guide to answer pressing questions.

The goal of this book is to provide you with an easy way to look at four different business cultures. Will Brazilians act the same as Russians? Not exactly. But, with an understanding of underlying business preferences, an American can get started on the right foot with engagements. Over time, each side of the business relationship will learn to understand how to work together; where we most often lose our footing is in our inability to even get started. This book will help you with that process.

BRIC Fast Facts

- Russia occupies 1/7th of the world's land.
- BRIC countries held their first summit in June 2008. They have met every year since that time to discuss how to corporate.
- China and India already boast 500 million Internet users expecting to grow to 700 million by 2015
- Europe has 35 cities with a population over 1 million people.
  –By 2030 India will have 68 cities with over 1 million people.
  –China will have over 1 billion people living in cities by 2030.
- Russia is the world's second largest oil exporter. Majority of Europe's energy needs are met by Russia.
- Brazil topped the BRIC with a growth rate of 8.9% for first half of 2010

CHAPTER 2:
THE AMERICAN EXPERIENCE

Most Americans are now expected to be Desk Diplomats without the experience of being an expatriate. We learn American business models in school with the assumption that all countries adopt the same business practices. This belief is reinforced by the fact that America, as a country, has been unbelievably successful when compared with others over the last century. Our success has been credited to our business culture and therefore management practices.

These beliefs leave us at a disadvantage when we need to do business with the BRIC because their business culture and expectations are different from ours. Americans are further disadvantaged by our experiences doing business in America. We interact with people on a daily basis who come from different cultures but have adopted American beliefs and business practices. Exposure to new Americans with their accented English is commonplace inside large organizations. We are the only country in the world with an immigrant population that, for the most part, is interested in adopting our culture.

These experiences, in some situations happening daily, dull our senses. When interacting with a Russian, we subconsciously expect the same actions and beliefs when doing business with an American Russian who lives in our community. This experience is not slight. Understanding this expectation is critical.

Over the past decade there has been a lot of talk about how global business has forced everyone to do business in the same way. This is not the case. Understanding this fact combined with the power of your daily experience will allow you to shift your expectations to align with a complex global work environment. The ability to start thinking big on a global level with all of its complications will heighten your ability to work across cultures. It will also have the added benefit of making you an important player in your organization.

Chapter 3:
A Very Short Introduction
to the BRIC

The BRIC is made up of four countries with different resources. Brazil and Russia offers raw materials and agriculture, while China and India are more focused on manufactured goods. This wide swath of business interests points to a high chance of engagement with the BRIC no matter what specialty your organization offers.

Jim O'Neil, head of economic research for Goldman Sachs, coined the term "BRIC" at the start of the 21st century. His research led him to predict that by 2050, these four countries will have combined economies that surpass the G7. In a recent interview, he changed the date of his prediction to 2035, noting that, with the exception of Russia, the global economic crisis had little impact on the BRIC, while the rest of the world is, at best, treading water. For more information on the BRIC, search for Goldman Sachs BRIC; the company's website offers a comprehensive section with video, presentations and statistics.

3.1 Why the BRIC Matters to YOU

I tell my clients or anyone else who asks, "Is outsourcing here to stay?" that the answer is yes, but it's only part of the change happening in the world. Americans outsourced for the cheap labor and time zone acceleration, but we really got interested when we realized that the employees we hired needed everything under the sun, from cars to banking services to insurance and anything else you can't imagine living without.

O'Neil predicts that by 2027, 70% of the world's car sales will be from the BRIC. In fact, just looking at auto sales alone is mind blowing. From 2008 to 2009, auto sales in China increased by 92%. And this happened while the rest of the world experienced a debilitating economy.

The best way I can describe what I have seen with my own eyes is that it's like someone flipped on the switch in the BRIC. The switch to decide: Yes, we want the things that others have and we want them now.

If your firm sells products or services, targeting the BRIC will be in your path to sustained growth because there is nowhere else to go for this kind of expansion. Procter and Gamble recently revealed in its earnings reports 12% growth in emerging markets including double digit growth in China. Morgan Stanley has suggested that by the end of this decade the number of people living in the BRIC with disposable incomes over $10,000 will surpass the US and Eurozone combined with a membership of 200 million people. This number, which seems so low, is actually stricter than most statistics that use $3,000 per annum on middle class projections. It's not hard to get to big numbers in the BRIC; it's where half of the world's population resides.

CHAPTER 4:
INTRODUCTION TO BUSINESS
CULTURAL PREFERENCES

Culture is what makes us subconsciously decide what is right and wrong, and what is appropriate. Without culture, day-to-day questions we think nothing about would become overwhelming to manage. From greeting those around us and deciding where to sit at a business dinner, to knowing how to treat a boss we see outside of the office, culture guides our journey through life. With the rise of globalization, being more culturally aware is becoming a skill rather than an experience. The number of cultures with which we interact is growing, and most of us will never have the opportunity to visit the culture long enough to truly understand how things are different.

In the Netherlands, a small country surrounded by the United Kingdom, France and Germany, the need to understand how to work across cultures begins at a young age in school where students learn Dutch and English, and get to choose German or French as a third language. The expression "go Dutch" is known across the world as a way of accommodating or meeting half way. This thinking spanned researchers in the Netherlands to spend their lives studying how cultures are different. Geert Hofstede, who worked with IBM over a 30-year period, developed a set of cultural dimensions that can be used to describe different cultural preferences. These ideas were enhanced and challenged by Fons Trompenaars. These ideas as well as other researchers including Edward Hall and Richard Lewis will be used in this book to give an introduction to the business cultural differences that are important for understanding how to work with the BRIC.

This book looks at five cultural factors that I consider to be critical for getting business done.

1. Communication Styles: How Organizations Communicate
2. Organizational Structure: How Decisions Are Managed
3. Power Distance: How Power Is Distributed
4. Individual vs. Group: How Employees Work Together
5. Relationship vs. Venture: How Organizations Engage Partners

These are core principles that make corporations work internally and externally. Across these five principles, the BRIC prefers the same things.

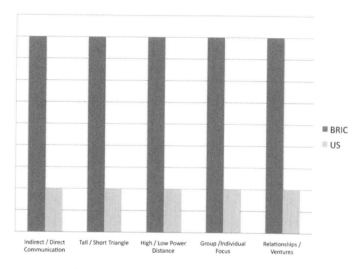

4.1 AIM Process: Three Steps to Cross-Cultural Success

Having an understanding of the differences, or intercultural sensitivity, only gets you so far. This sensitivity, typically taught in the form of cross-cultural training, gives you a feeling of the differences but it rarely does a great job of telling you how to convert feelings into actions. Organizations need Desk Diplomats who can turn understanding into action. One of our nation's biggest concerns is how to transition our talent into a global workforce.

I developed a simple framework to answer this problem called AIM: Assess, Identify and Mediate.

This framework walks Americans through the process of understanding themselves from a distance, identifying how their business culture preferences are different from the partner, and transforming this information into a mediation plan for action. It's a cycle that can be used again and again when engaging with new business cultures.

AIM offers clear insights into how business partners are different, a critical factor in starting relationships on the right foot. The frustration clients often have is due to a lack of clarity on how the problems started. Unfortunately, this conversation often happens after a product is delivered late, which is a symptom of problems that have been growing unchecked for months. By decoding differences, a roadmap can be formed guiding teams around problems that would create unfavorable outcomes.

4.2. Assess

The first part of the AIM process is an assessment of home business culture preferences. It's difficult to recognize your own business culture preferences because they are ingrained as well as used on a daily basis. This book focuses on five cultural factors. Americans are generalized as holding similar values in these areas, which are covered in detail in the following pages:

1. Communication Styles: US prefers direct communication
2. Organizational Structure: US prefers flat organizations
3. Power Distance: US has low power distance
4. Individual vs. Group: US focuses on individual goals
5. Relationship vs. Venture: US focuses on venture

Note: In the majority of cases, it's safe to use generalizations about Americans, but for a corporation or individual that wants to become a true global master, doing an in-depth profile is the answer. We offer these online at TheGlobalManager.com/CultureCompetencyProfile. See coupon at back of book for a discount code.

The worst mistake American managers make is assuming that first generations are the right candidate to put on a cross-culture project. They think, his parents are from Russia, so let's send him! Often, first generations have little to no experience with their parents' country of origin. They may have seen it as a tourist, but this experience does not heighten their skills for business. And pitching them to the partner team as a good candidate because "their parents are from your country" sends a bad message.

*A friend in India said it well: "Tell them to stop sending the first "gens," the **gundā** are better." **Gundā** is a moniker for white people in India as well as a slang word used to describe hoodlums. If you make a first-generation choice, regardless of background, do it for language. Brazilians speak a slightly different Portuguese than those from Portugal. A speaker of Russian or Chinese will also be powerful to engage in the project (but make sure they speak the right Chinese language, there are more than you think: Mandarin, Cantonese, Dungan, Gan, Hakka, Shanghainese, Taiwanese, Teochew and Xiang) but avoid assigning leadership to this person unless it's appropriate.*

4.3 Identify

The second step of the AIM framework is identify. By spending time identifying differences, Americans can engage across the BRIC in a way that will be the most powerful: like locals. One of the highest compliments that can be paid to an American (who will always fight the image of America that is played out in movies and television) is for a BRIC counterpart to say "you have worked with us before then" or "it seems like you are from here."

The BRIC preferences discussed in this book are listed below.
1. Communication Styles: BRIC prefers indirect communication
2. Organizational Structure: BRIC prefers hierarchical structures
3. Power Distance: BRIC prefers high power distance between managers and subordinates
4. Individual vs. Group: BRIC prefers focus on group
5. Relationship vs. Task: BRIC prefers focus on relationships

An in-depth review of business culture differences can be found in Chapter 5.

Inside corporations, cross-culturally savvy people can be hiding, and often bosses have no idea who is the most culturally competent. One group that is often overlooked is Army brats. The children of Army parents are constantly moved, causing them to become more culturally sensitive in their youth. As the new kid on the block, they had to learn the local rules and figure out how to get into the right group. They carry this skill into adulthood, even if they stayed in the US, and will manage cross-cultural communication with more ease.

> *Engaging in cross-cultural understanding is similar to men and women trying to understand each other within a marriage. Men try to understand their wives and ask for guidance while women seek to do the same with their husbands.*

4.4 Mediate

The last step in the AIM process is mediation, where leaders work to find a common language for engagement by leveraging the information they know about their own business culture preferences and how these differ from the potential partner. With my clients, this takes place live in

the training room, in a consulting assignment or during a coaching session. For you, this process will take place here in chapters 6-8 where mediation strategies are presented throughout a list of activities that you will encounter throughout your partnership with the BRIC. Each section will help you get on the right road to figuring out what is happening in the minds on the other side of the table.

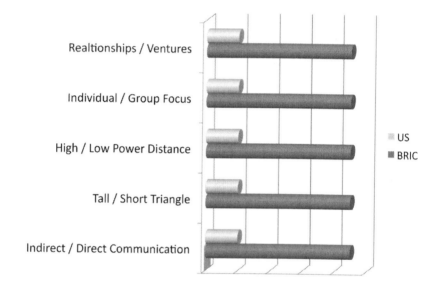

Chapter 5:
The Five Business Culture Preferences

When we engage new partners from the BRIC, there are five preferences that impact our abilities to be successful as we attempt to develop commitment across teams to produce successful projects. This section covers these factors in detail taking an in-depth look at how the BRIC compares to US:

1. Communication Styles: How Organizations Communicate
2. Organizational Structure: How Decisions Are Managed
3. Power Distance: How Power Is Distributed
4. Individual vs. Group: How Employees Work Together
5. Relationship vs. Task: How Organizations Engage Partners

5.1 Communication Styles

Communication is the foundation of any cross-cultural relationship, making it an important topic to cover first. The way people communicate inside the same culture is defined as high or low context.

One of the reasons low-context cultures exist is because there is extensive diversity inside the culture, making it difficult to develop high-context signals that everyone understands. In America, the rich diversity of groups requires a unique intensity of low-context and direct communication. The popularity of our movies and TV programs around the world is a testament to low context. For the most part, anyone can understand the messages. Meaning is relayed by the use of words rather than environment or other high-context messaging routes. The use of informal communication is rampant, elders are given some status as well as bosses, but Americans hold no recourse in stating opinions to these groups. There is a feeling that everything must be said and that everyone is open to hearing messages stated in a work environment.

This makes phrases like "frankly" or "don't take this personally" or "to be honest" useful because there are few alternatives to send messages beyond speech. From the outside, Americans can appear to be blunt, rude and inappropriate. We miss signals because we don't know to look for them when working across cultures.

The BRIC countries prefer high-context communication. High-context cultures are formal communicators and prefer indirect communication. The use of Dr. and Mr. are prevalent, and deference is given to the eldest of the group. High-context cultures think of the group before the individual, making it important to deliver messages that do not offend because there is a need to save face and give face to leadership. BRIC countries send messages that may need to be decoded, such as telling a story that appears to be irrelevant to the situation. It's not. The story has a meaning that is important.

High-context cultures can be disarming to those not prepared to "listen loudly." In the BRIC, listening goes beyond reading and hearing words and includes observing voice tone, timing, body language and message location. After listening loudly to all of these things, the communication as a whole can be evaluated. When working with the BRIC, high-context styles are made more difficult to understand because counterparts are using a second language. The ability to express in English is difficult in its use as a second language. Indians, who learn English at a young age in the upper classes of society, still grapple with expressing meanings in English relative to their native Hindi or local language. The same is true for Brazilians who speak Portuguese, which offers a lot of subtleties in verbal communication by the use of hierarchical pronouns. English does not offer the same level of verboseness and formal messaging.

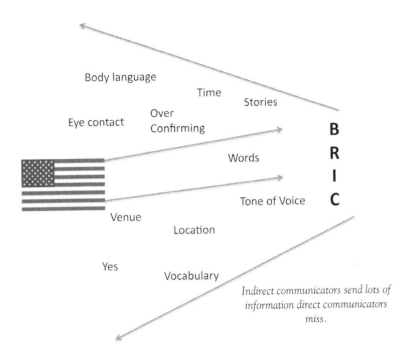

Body language
Time
Stories
Eye contact
Over
Confirming
Words
Venue
Location
Yes
Vocabulary
Tone of Voice

B
R
I
C

Indirect communicators send lots of information direct communicators miss.

When high-context and low-context communicators meet, trouble can arise in business relationships. While there is a worldwide understanding of American directness, this does not mean it works for Desk Diplomats. The best advice for Americans on high-context interactions is to think about interactions with their mothers, fathers, siblings or significant others. Consider a phone conversation with one of these people that resulted in questions after hanging up: What were they really trying to say? This is the closest understanding Americans have to high-context communication. This closeness and understanding exists inside organizations across the BRIC.

When Americans ask themselves these questions, a high-context problem has been presented:

Q: Why is this communication happening now?
A: Timing is everything in high-context communications. Don't rely on an URGENT subject line.

Q: Are they repeating my question instead of answering it?
A: Over confirmations are ways of asking you to make a different choice.

Q: Are you answering a question with "of course it is?"
A: By asking questions where the answer is already known, this person is actually asking for a different answer or needs more information.

Q: Is the story relevant to something?
A: All stories are relevant and convey a message. Ask questions about the story and answers will reveal themselves.

Q: Does body language match interest?
A: When interacting in person, be aware of body language. Most intuitions will signal a need to take a second look at what is happening.

5.2 Organizational Structure

An organization's structure is a combination of culture and need. Culture preferences are typically selected by default, based on headquarter preferences, while need relates to industry type.

In the US, organizations have moved away from tall-triangle organizational structures, which were popular over the last century. In tall triangles, decisions are made at the top and pushed down through multiple levels of management. Tasks, not responsibilities, are assigned with specific details on how to carry them out. Your grandfather, if he was American, worked inside a tall-triangle organization where employees followed the boss's orders while understanding that the boss was looking out for them. This model existed beyond the factory floor illustrated in "The Producers" where Matthew Broderick begins the movie as an accountant who toils away under the harsh direction of the boss. Broderick is a knowledge worker, but he is specifically directed in how to use that knowledge. Triangles continue to exist in the US, but most are found in factory environments where safety is more important than creativity.

Tall Triangle   Flat Organizations

As workplace needs shifted in the US, triangles flattened into rectangular hierarchies where, in most situations, decisions are made at the top, but ideas are also pushed up for confirmation. This is prevalent in today's companies. Your manager assigns you a responsibility with the expectation that you will determine the right path to get it done. In America, it is possible to campaign an idea across several stakeholders and then push up to get a final approval.

The BRIC's preference for hierarchy creates problems for those accustomed to working with flat organizations. I find the factory floor analogy to be powerful. Consider how specific everyone in the factory is with his role and responsibility. This is exactly what you should expect inside the BRIC even if it's a knowledge environment. Roles are clearly defined. Responsibilities are laid out specifically for subordinates and management. If something falls outside of this box, it is someone else's task or decision. Tall-triangle environments encourage different behaviors and can sideline Americans who expect environments with less structure and a whatever-it–takes-to-get-the-job-done mentality.

When Americans ask themselves these questions, hierarchy is likely to blame:

Q: Why is this decision taking so long to make?
A: *Layers of hierarchy add time to decision-making. Include time for answers to be disseminated from management.*

Q: Why is the person with whom I've been working suddenly ignoring me?
A: *The person you have engaged is too low in the hierarchy to participate in the conversation. Move to engage at a higher level in the organization.*

Q: I thought we solved this problem?

A: Communication around the problem likely happened with someone at too low a level for decision-making. He may have agreed with you but could not cement the agreement without consent of the boss.

Q: I set up a meeting, but now that I have traveled to the BRIC why are my attempts to connect being ignored?

A: Someone at a higher level in the organization needed to approve the meeting.

Q: How does the boss know everything?

A: Bosses are expected to know all the answers in tall triangles. Those in the organization strive to push information to the top so the boss never loses face when questions are posed. For Americans, this requires a fine balance of educating those lower in the organization and not wasting time with those without decision- making authority.

5.3 Power Distance

The way power is distributed in societies and organizations is measured by power distance. In American culture, we have low power distance but not as low as some northern European countries. Cultures such as Denmark have such low power distance that leaders engage in common activities, such as visiting an ATM machine or bank. Americans would be surprised to see our president engaging in these everyday tasks. Can you imagine a bank that wouldn't come directly to the president for his business? Didn't think so.

In low power distance environments, managers and their subordinates are closer to equal. Those below managers have decision-making authority and are expected to develop creative approaches for the responsibilities assigned to them. Americans push responsibilities forward by working informally across groups. The person responsible will discover the best way to get things done. They can informally work for one manager on a project while reporting to another.

As previously discussed, BRIC organizations have high power distance through tall triangles. But power distance goes beyond organizational hierarchy; it creates structures where employees are unequal from management. This inequality is displayed in all aspects of the organization, including the ability to make decisions, having a big-picture understanding of a project, and having access to information. Power distance enhances the need to save face; everyone plays a part in keeping established roles in check.

Power distance is the biggest problem in US relationships with the BRIC. Americans should take heed of one piece of advice: work directly with decision makers. An employee low in the hierarchy has little ability to suggest ideas to the boss. This creates a possible loss of face. Unless the employee is an intermediary and can immediately bring the issue to the top of the organization, starting a conversation at the wrong level can kill an idea. Project managers are most affected by differing power distance because indirect leadership doesn't work. All of the skills that work well in the US fall on the floor because decisions are not made by peers, and peers can't bring ideas to their boss.

When Americans ask themselves these questions, power distance is likely to blame:

Q: The project manager I am working with told me this was ok. Why is this manager now changing things around?
A: The project manager did not have the power to make the decision. Make sure you have a decision by asking for implementation details.

Q: Why doesn't anyone speak on the conference calls except the manager?
A: In BRIC cultures, the manager speaks for the team at all times.

Q: I just arrived at the office to meet with my contact but people are not sure why I am here. I thought this was an idea they were interested in?
A: Setting up a meeting with the wrong person is common because someone at your level may not be able to make decisions. Work with decision makers.

5.4 Individual vs Group

Americans live in an individual-focused culture, one of the most individually focused in the world. Our ancestors were frontiers who left behind family allegiances and obligations to be part of the American dream. Those just arriving in America have the same trait: to leave what you know behind requires individual rather than group focus. My grandmother refuses to speak about her past in Spain and why her parents left. She did not teach my mother Spanish because her goal was to assimilate into American culture. Many Americans have similar stories to this one.

Our parents raise us to be self-sufficient from a very young age. Parents encourage us to speak up for ourselves as early as possible. Think about the children you know who are unable to read but order their own dinner after discussing the menu with their parents. In kindergarten, children engage in show and tell presenting to the class something they are passionate about. American society identifies with characters that go beyond the group and seek individual pursuits and dreams. Think about the last movie you watched, does this sound familiar? We have heroes in our culture like Superman who is the ultimate individual sent by his parents to a new world alone. When Superman has problems he escapes to an ice castle in the far north and reflects alone.

Over the past century, Americans have moved away from working for the same company to focusing on enhancing their own resume by seeking out jobs, education and other roles that are part of an individualized career roadmap. This shift has accelerated at warp speed over the last 10 years with many people leaving Corporate America altogether to become independent consultants who offer highly specialized skills to organizations at a specific time of need. Without the home base of a corporation, Americans have turned to themselves to construct the right opportunities at the right time.
Job descriptions attract the "right" person to solve an organization's problems rather than the organization seeking to grow employees into the required roles. Promotions are granted on effort and given out

randomly rather than according to a specific timeline. Americans work in an achievement focused business culture where merits are handed out based on accomplishments rather than an ascription culture, preferred by the BRIC, where companies select potential leaders and push them through the organization on a planned roadmap to leadership.

This business culture leads Americans to be constantly thinking about initiatives in terms of their own growth and achievement. We ask ourselves what is the best way to get this done and how have I done this successfully before without regard to others involved in the situation. From that point, we question initiatives and bring our propositions to the table. This is organizational design, and Americans are rewarded when they excel inside it. Managers in US companies expect employees to offer these skills and rate them highly when they guide an objective to success outside of the box the organization initially laid out. Experience is so highly valued inside Corporate America that it is very rare in the 21st century to meet someone who has worked for a firm for more than 10 years. This is especially prevalent inside communities where innovation is a focus. Technology companies shun applicants who work at the same firm for long periods of time, aligning with the American belief that employee growth and development cannot happen inside the same organization. Experiences must come from different places.

The BRIC countries are collectivist, or focused on the good of the group. Employees work to enhance the status of the organization and their bosses. Decisions are not based on how they impact the employee, although being involved with positive action is not shied away from. Instead, focus is on how the group can be bettered by action. This creates strong teams composed of individuals who consider it their responsibility to not leave anyone on the team behind.

Teams in collectivist cultures form strong in-groups similar to the in-groups that exist in families. When the in-group is considered the highest order, employees act and react differently. The true root of a problem may never be discovered because the team takes on the responsibility for problems. Individuals in these groups can feel a strong sense of shame creating situations where employees take drastic action such as suicide. This happened recently at an Apple iPhone manufacturer in China. Employees want to avoid causing the organization shame at any cost.

> *When working with group cultures, avoid using American training techniques that ask if anyone knows the answer. Instead, create groups to answer questions.*

When Americans ask themselves these questions, individual vs. group behavior is likely to blame:

Q: Why is my contact suddenly acting so strangely? They are not returning calls and their work is atrocious.

A: Americans have functional attribution error when interacting with the BRIC. Because of our individual approach, we see others' actions as related only to them rather than the larger picture of the group. Investigate what is really happening by engaging someone higher in the organization and reviewing communications for indirect messages.

Q: Someone on this team is causing all of these problems ... but who is it?

A: You may never find out. The group will defend as well as react to problems internally. Trust the group to root out and fix the problem.

Q: Doesn't this guy see this is an unbelievable opportunity for his career?

A: Americans strive for their own career and take a job because it fits into a larger personal plan. This is not the case in the BRIC. The good of the group will be considered first.

5.5 Relationships vs Ventures

When decisions are made in business environments, considerations focus on the venture and/or relationships. Focusing on the venture is related to abilities the partner offers while focusing on the relationship is about the people the partner brings to the engagement. In the US, we are taught to build a better mousetrap and the world will be at your door. This ingrained idea teaches us that the best offering should always win. When offerings are similar, price is then considered. The way we approach business in the US is focused on our offering rather than who stands beside it. This is not to say that people do not prefer to do business with those they like; this is, of course, preferred. But we will most often pick the best offering over the person offering something considered weaker and "deal" with those that accompany it.

In the BRIC the primary driver behind business is relationships.

Businesses are focused on building networks of the right relationships to ensure access. When starting a project, it would be natural to reach out to those you know and ask for introductions rather than reaching out to the world to see what is offered. This makes the relationships inside business dealings important. When these individuals are replaced, the relationship may be terminated, **even one with a contract**. As a Desk Diplomat, it's important to understand this at the start of a project. The BRIC will be interested in getting to know you and retaining ties with whoever brought the partnership to the table in the first place. Americans cannot win on data points alone in the BRIC; they need to spend time building relationships.

We like to think we spend time on relationships but they often come second to getting things done. We value time in the United States in a way that others don't understand. We put a value on time, making time equal to money and sending us into a constant pursuit of saving it. When building an international relationship, pursing timesaving strategies is a venture-focused strategy. Open your schedule to the BRIC by making time for relationships to develop. Don't shut down conversations because of time. It's critical that you develop a strong relationship with your BRIC colleagues.

Because of our individualism, Americans have many "faces." This term, first suggested by Edward T. Hall, shows how Americans have the capability of playing many roles inside one society. This means we don't need to carry identities with us everywhere we go. An American may be the boss at work but a player on the work baseball team. He may be friendly with a couple that has children of the same age but never invite these friends into his closer social circle of intimate friends. He may be a deacon at the local church but have no relationship with congregation members at work. Because we have many slices, it's possible for us to have an identity that goes beyond work or our other roles. With these additional identities we create a wall between our personal self and the self who goes to work every day. To be criticized at work is not to be criticized at home.

In the BRIC, life has fewer slices. The role played at work is the same role held everywhere else in the community. The boss is the boss wherever he is encountered and must be shown deference. All aspects of his life align with the leadership position.

This difference creates complications for Americans when developing relationships because the questions the BRIC asks seem inappropriate. I am sure you know someone who has been invited to something considered very intimate in US culture by someone in the BRIC. An Indian wedding may come to mind. Keep in mind that this is how the BRIC works. Be open to discussing things that your American colleagues may not ask.

> *Sending a delegate to represent an American company must be well thought out before departure. This delegate must have authority as well as longevity in the organization. Replacing delegates during the relationship should be done with care and planning. The new contact will need to be brought in slowly to transition the relationship. It is wise for American firms to engage more than one delegate to a relationship with the BRIC or they risk the business leaving with a delegate who departs.*

CHAPTER 6:
ENGAGING WITH THE BRIC

Now that you know more about how the US and the BRIC differ, we transition into the most important part of being a Desk Diplomat: taking action. Organizations need action. They need global workers who make projects successful by moving beyond understanding cultural differences to using these skills to bring projects to successful fruition.

This section reviews how US and BRIC cultural preferences play out inside common workplace activities. From daily activities such as conference calls to meeting planning, it will serve as a reference when you engage during your workday. To be able to act on what you understand is the differentiator between being a leader and a global leader. It takes practice and may feel uncomfortable at first. Give the suggestions a try and develop your own based on your results.

6.1 What to Expect When Getting Started

One of the most complicated things about starting a relationship with the BRIC from the US is that you often were not the individual who blazed the initial path to develop the partnership. In the US, deals are done and then assigned to those who can implement. This is not the case in the BRIC. In the BRIC there is extensive discussions about who, what, where, when and how before a contract is signed. This is a problem for you because it's likely you were not involved in any of these initial discussions, making you late to the game.

Your first goal is to discover what has already been discussed and decided. This information exists somewhere. Find it. It could be in the contract, appendices or with someone on the BRIC side who documented conversations. Ask if there were discussions before you joined the team and review them before engaging. Take seriously whatever decisions were made, the BRIC will operate under the impression that these decisions are final.

When setting the first meeting, gather information for an agenda, and get a handle on the roles and responsibilities of everyone involved. Enter the first call in a way that demonstrates authority but openness to listening and accepting new information. Avoid causing loss of face for yourself or your team by saying things like "would have been nice to have" or "wish they would have told us that."

Project Managers often come into these situations with a strict reference on the PMI Book of Knowledge and try to begin its implementation. Proceed with caution. Most countries do not use the Book of Knowledge in the same way as the US, if at all. Sitting across from someone with a PMI certification does not mean they are well versed in your business methods. Spend some time figuring out what methods work best and recognize that some situations may call for less formal approaches to make the project work.

A project manager for a large corporation in Brazil recently told me that the PMI Book of Knowledge is used infrequently at best inside Brazilian projects. He also warned against assuming that someone with a PMI certification has extensive experience, as is the case in the US.

6.2 Meeting Planning

No two meetings are the same but they all need a plan. When engaging the BRIC, the plan must consider the different facets of business culture and how they show up at the table.

When working with the BRIC, the biggest decision is if having a group discussion is the best path. In cultures where saving face is a concern, the art of tactically hedging around a problem and not placing blame is a skill Desk Diplomats must learn. Think carefully before setting up a call that may feel like an inquisition to the BRIC team. If the goal is to discuss a problem and you already know what the problem is, ask the manager to give you some feedback. He may go to the team directly to get answers, but you have not caused him to lose face. Also consider if engaging your boss is a better option. The higher the title the more importance the BRIC will give the conversation. If the decision is to have the call, construct a list of people who need to be on the call. Ask the manager who should be involved and include him on every call. If he is not going to attend, ask for a delegate, but be warned that no decisions will be made without him. If the goal of the call is to record project status, be sure to understand who can report. If you get the team on the phone without the manager, problems may arise.

In tall-triangle environments with high power distance, meetings are used to discuss decisions already made. Opinions held by subordinates that go against decisions will not be expressed. Avoid scheduling meetings that create forums for causing loss of face by accepting decisions that come from the BRIC as they are without drawing a group of people into a meeting who have little to say about them. You will lose face if you try to bring a discussion about "how dumb an idea is" to the BRIC. The BRIC will protect its' bosses vigorously. Instead, talk to the decision maker directly.

The BRIC prefers to spend a lot of time upfront establishing details before kicking off the project. This is the opposite of the US practice of signing a contract and figuring out the details later. You may be running meetings that don't seem serious because all of the contracts have not been signed. Ignore this feeling and be aware that contracts will never come to fruition unless all of the details are established.

Agendas are a great process for trying to figure out what might be presented at a meeting. Soliciting agenda items from the right people on the BRIC side is a good way to catalog issues and get organized. Make sure you engage the right person on the BRIC side to get this information, specifically the manager. If you are a project manager working with another project manager, understand that the BRIC project manager doesn't have the authority you have: bosses make decisions. The project manager may not be able to do anything but report. If you need to discuss decisions, engage the boss directly.

The timing of meetings will be different. Give yourself extra time at the end, keeping in mind that the discussion will not fit into the typical US one-hour meeting. Over time, both sides will learn what works best for the team. Limiting conversation to one hour may not work, but not using time well will also fail. As you engage, find an accommodation such as asking the team to be mindful of time constraints at most

meetings and letting others run long. Once you have an agenda, consider it a framework for the meeting rather than an absolute. In the BRIC cultures, agendas are helpful, but many meetings unfold in a different way than is predicted by an agenda.

See also: Preparing and Running Conference Calls, Using and Finding an Intermediary, Using a Translator

If this is the first meeting with the potential partner, work hard to make sure you have an appointment. Plan many weeks in advance and ask for written confirmation of the appointment three times by sending a friendly email that includes a specific question to answer. This begins the process of building a relationship from afar while engaging the contact in making the appointment happen. I have flown around the world for meetings that are suddenly canceled. Have faith! Usually once you are local, they take you more seriously and will find a way to make a meeting work.

6.3 Preparing and Running Conference Calls

You might be wondering why this section talks about conference calls when we just talked about meeting planning. Use the meeting planning process for conference calls but also review these specifics. Conference calls add an additional layer of complexity when working across cultures. The primary reason is obvious: we can't see each other! When we can't see each other, reading indirect communication and high-context signals becomes impossible.

Conference calls in the US are a place for gathering information and making decisions. An agenda is used to map out the call and determine who is going to speak about what. They are timed precisely and the strength of a call is measured by how efficiently it is run. The rigid nature of time in the US workplace forces conversations that would naturally take longer to be tabled and handled by email or sent to a decision maker.

BRIC countries do not have conference calls to make decisions. Their intention is to report decisions and discuss the details of implementation.

- In China, having such an open discussion is not welcome.
- In Brazil, conference calls are used to emphasize new insights with a lot of discussion and enthusiasm on new data. Managers make the decisions after robust discussions are completed.
- In India, managers answer all questions and typically make next step decisions after the call. Subordinates may listen in but do not participate.
- Russians are capable of being very direct, sounding decisive during calls, but ultimately decisions lie with managers.

Communication style in the US is low context, but this can come across as strong, loud and bitingly direct on a conference call. Without visuals, tone of voice and choice of words are the only tools that can be used to understand each other. When the BRIC come to the call, they are hit with using a second language in a style with which they are uncomfortable. These cultures are accustomed to sending messages with less focus on words and more focus on timing, location, and body language.

Our differences with communication create two specific problems inside conference calls: floor control mismanagement and inaccurate interpretation of data sent from the BRIC side.

Floor control is defined as the speaker at any given moment, or the owner of the floor. In the US, floor control is up for grabs, as Americans jump in and offer information, often interrupting each other to get their voices heard. In the BRIC, control of the floor is more organized through the use of signals and roles.

In the BRIC, the manager is usually the voice of the team. The manager may answer questions while subordinates busy themselves with other activities. Avoid asking an individual contributor directly for information; this will cause the manager and the employee to lose face. If the manager needs the information, he can directly engage the employee.

Most speakers will be leveraging English as a second language, making it difficult to understand pauses and entry points. Without some kind of verbal signal such as eye contact or other body language, it's challenging to determine whose turn it is. Think about the last time you were on a conference call and accidentally started talking at the same time as someone way above you. Whoops. This problem is magnified because more formality is expected in the BRIC.

It's important to give the BRIC plenty of time – which to you may seem like painful silence – to engage. Silence is avoided in the US; Americans like to jump in when they encounter silence. Don't jump in. Instead formally ask the other side to answer and then wait. There may be what feels like an extensive delay before they respond to you. Russians are an exception to this; they tend to be more aggressive than the rest of the BRIC. Once you have mastered floor control, you will be amazed at the difference. It will feel like the team is working together from thousands of miles away.

After overcoming the obstacles of floor control, the next problem that comes to the forefront is harmony. In cultures with high power distance, tall-triangle structures and a preference for relationships rather than ventures, behavior towards others on a conference call is similar to engaging with family members. This presents a few problems.

- **More time will be needed to greet everyone.** In fact, don't be surprised if each member of the team wants to say 'hi' to everyone else. This can last for 15 minutes if you don't find a way to control the situation. I suggested to one client that they let the whole team greet each other all at once and then leave 10 minutes at the end of the meeting for a select few people to give an update and individually relay greetings. These people are rotated in and out over the course of the project. This keeps the BRIC team on schedule and allows relationships to develop. It also gives the Americans a chance to think about something personal they want to share.

- **It is preferable to give positive answers in the BRIC**, such as "yes" and "we can do it," even when it is not the case. Follow up on any positive responses to take on additional items with questions about the details. This should help root out if a proposal is real. Don't count on voice enthusiasm to guide you: this is how we typically read truth. The truth is the BRIC wants to please the partner.

> *Tip: Remember, slow down the call, allowing for long pauses in responses to allow the BRIC time to gather thoughts, translate them and send them back.*

See also: Meeting Planning, Using and Finding an Intermediary, Using a Translator, Recognizing Sincerity

6.4 Managing Communication Technologies

Virtual teams inside the US are difficult to manage but pushing this location boundary to include the BRIC adds high-context communication, high power distance and group orientation ... a recipe for disaster for the unaware. Here is an overview of the points for Desk Diplomats:

Instant messaging / Twitter-type platforms: Remember that English is a second language for the BRIC cultures, causing a translation delay. It's also direct, individual communication. Avoid using instant communication methods to ask someone other than the manager a direct question about status, etc. This will force the person you are speaking with to either ignore you or have to ask the manager for the answer.

Some of my clients have started using internal Twitter platforms that allow people to search conversations at a later date. This is a workable solution if you are talking about information people need to access. Remember that cultures with high power distance don't share as much information. Rather, information is power so it's withheld from others. Find the right balance for sharing information.

Wiki: Using Wiki is effective inside complex projects. The first step is to outline in detail what should be on the Wiki even if all of the information isn't available at the moment. Outlining intention is important because it eliminates the fear of asking for information: It's clear that it's supposed to be available making it a lot easier to ask. Americans are then forced to be more detailed. When working with  the BRIC, US managers will encounter things that seem simple or unspoken but need to be documented in detail. I have worked with managers who say, "Why do they need such detailed instructions?" This is how these business cultures work. They are accustomed to having managers who assign tasks and outline in great detail what needs to be done.

Email: I encourage teams to follow strict rules when using email. Email, while extremely effective from a lot of vantages, is a minefield in cross-cultural relationships.

- **Time zone considerations**. Remember that most of the BRIC, with the exception of Brazil, lives about a half-day ahead of us. If it takes them few hours to return an email, the day is literally gone.

- **Strike out at three times**. If you are still trying to get an answer after going around three times in email, stop and assess. Are you asking the right person? Is this person using high-context communication to tell you something? Think. Then decide whom you are going to call to get an answer. Is it the manager? The person you are about to respond to? Make decisions and take action.
- **Interpreting long, detailed emails**. When cultures are tuned to high-context communication, they fall short when confronted with the written word as a sole vehicle of communication. When reading emails that are long, try to decipher what they are really trying to say. It's estimated that it takes Indians 2.7 times as long to say the same thing in English as it would an American. If they received a direct message, imagine that they are trying to keep harmony and use a story to send a message. The BRIC will tell stories that have meaning in emails that may puzzle you. Think about what they might really be trying to say.

Get on the PHONE! It's really cheap to call the BRIC. I called Brazil last week and it was 21 cents a minute. You can talk for an hour and cost your organization just 12 dollars. This is an insignificant sum compared with wasting days on email cycles that delay decisions.

When you use the phone, you build personal relationships. Hearing the voice on the other side of the phone is much different than email. Make a habit to get on the phone with your contacts in the BRIC; it will build relationships for the long term.

See also: Managing Information, Recognizing Sincerity

6.5 The Mystery of Face

Americans have a hard time understanding the BRIC's idea of losing face. The idea of face exists in regions that have a preference for the group over the individual, high power distance, high levels of hierarchy, and a relationship orientation. Its existence is enhanced by indirect or high-context communication. In other words, this is not a Chinese trait; other cultures beyond the BRIC, have an embedded concept of face.

Nothing like it exists in our culture. Nothing. I cannot stress this enough to Americans: We never lose face. Being embarrassed is not losing face. Embarrassment is a guilt feeling not a shame feeling. We exist in a direct culture where losing face is **almost impossible**. The level of separation Americans hold as a society that focuses on individual achievement eliminates the possibility. Unless you are working in an environment that is run by foreign managers or have parents from a culture that has face, losing face is not something you have experienced.

In a culture that has face, members are concerned about keeping their own face safe as well as those to whom they have claimed allegiance, such as a boss or another leader in the community. This is the up and down of saving face. It has two parts: saving and giving. In the BRIC, ascription is preferred where promotions are based on time served and education rather than achievements. Teams work to help the manger grow into the manger they ascribe him to be, rather than competing with him and others to take the position for themselves (as happens in the US and other achievement cultures). This creates an up and down cycle where the group will work hard as a unit to maintain integrity across itself and will defend other members if necessary through an ebb and flow of giving and saving face:

- The group works to educate the manager to be able to speak intelligently as he must always know the answer. (Giving face)
- Group members defend the allegiance to the manager to make sure they themselves appear to be with the right group, but this may require them to lose face personally. Taking the blame for leaders is expected in these societies. (Giving and saving face)
- The group takes the blame, giving face to their boss so he can continue to keep face. This is a loss to them but a gain because they continue to be with the right leader. (Giving and saving face)

Americans are confused by the ebb and flow of face. We rarely consider that someone is taking responsibility because that is expected, making it hard to get to the root of problems. We become frustrated when subordinates give face to the manager by always letting him be the expert in the room, even if he is wrong and someone knows better. In our culture the one that is right speaks up.

As a Desk Diplomat, trying to understand face is important. Some think face doesn't apply to the type of interactions you are performing, and they are wrong. Face, in its rawest form, causes teams to work together and defend the boss in an almost cult-like fashion. If a loss of face occurs, it may be impossible to reconcile. It would take an effort on your part to give face as well as require involving people at high levels in your organization. To avoid this:

- Understand that the manager must be propped up and supported at all costs. Avoid going direct to employees unless you are given authority to do so.
- Monitor behavior that seems evasive. Likely, the manager doesn't know the information you are requesting. Give him time to find out.
- Micromanagement is your friend in dealing with face cultures. It sets the tone from the start that you are a detail wizard, seeking out information at certain times from the team. This will prepare them to give you what you want when you want it.

See also: Recognizing Sincerity, Meeting Planning, Providing Feedback, Influencing Teams

Chapter 7.
Building Team Commitment

Building commitment is the core of a successful cross-cultural team. Several researchers have shown that multi-cultural teams can be more effective than mono-cultural teams. While this is easy to imagine -- differences across cultures develop new ideas -- it is difficult to bring to fruition without a focus on building commitment.

At the start, multi-cultural teams need to focus on building commitment. I have seen multi-cultural teams fail because they assumed team members will figure out how to work together but they did not consider cultural differences. The dominant culture may believe their management style is best, leaving little room for the other cultures to express their own gifts to the relationship.

Americans who focus on reconciling needs as well as building relationships inside diverse teams will build commitment by default. This section covers the following aspects of building commitment inside a cross-cultural team:
   a. Managing Time
   b. Managing Information
   c. Managing Decisions
   d. Providing Feedback
   e. Leading Indirectly
   f. Communicating Effectively
   g. Influencing Teams
   h. Developing Relationships
   i. Recognizing Sincerity

Desk Diplomats already have this skill set, but it needs to be adapted for a global audience who holds different business cultural preferences. Without understanding how to tweak skills that create streamlined teams, projects fail.

> *Problems arise in outsource relationships when Americans assume outsourcers will use American management styles and don't work on building commitment. When you hear people say, "they don't care about our project," this is an indicator of a team without commitment.*

7.1 Managing Time

Time in the American workplace is strictly managed. We hold one-hour meetings lead by an agenda. If a conversation lasts longer than the agenda allows, we table the discussion, push it to a vote to make a decision, or send the decision to a higher authority. In the US, time is money. There is a belief that time can be wasted or lost. This makes us constantly aware of how we are spending time and whether it is a worthwhile exercise.

Time is viewed differently across the BRIC. These cultures do not think of time as something that can be wasted. Inside organizations there is more time for discussions, relationships and to talk about details. Hard quarterly projections are not part of their culture. The feeling is that things will get done when they are supposed to.

When the BRIC works with us, they feel stifled by our need to keep everything in check time wise. This happens at meetings when we end the meeting on the hour and they feel that the discussion was just getting started. When creating products, our needs to meet a timeline may not be understood in the same way. A delay here and there is expected in these countries where it is much harder to be timely.

When working on a BRIC-based project from the US with limited ability to understand exactly what is happening at all times, our time differences clash. When engaging the BRIC in a project that requires delivery at certain points, you will need to set up a detailed schedule to check progress long before the actual due date. It's wise for managers to establish checkpoints to track progress. Don't wait until the day before to see how things are going, ask two weeks before. When you are asking, work on relationship building to establish trust. When the BRIC begins to trust you, they will see being in communication about possible delays as proactive. You may feel it is a waste of time to check in frequently, but it will root out problems early.

Show the BRIC the big picture. If you are able to share information on the complexity of projects, you will provide a greater understanding of timing. I worked with one team who had a master spreadsheet that was discussed point by point at each meeting with the BRIC team, illustrating how latency would impact the timetable. This was eye-opening to the team, who suddenly understood how their participation in the project impacted everything else.

Avoid thinking your contract is going to save you; it won't. I recently interviewed a lawyer for my column in *Outsource Magazine* who believes that timing clauses in contracts save projects. I disagree. Clauses will save money when the work needs to be redone or if the work is late, but clauses will not save the investment your corporation has made into the project. If your project has market timing and you miss being the first entrant, no contract clause will recoup the possible opportunity. Organizations lose hundreds of millions of dollars when they miss a market window.

See also: Meeting Planning, Preparing and Running Conference Calls

7.2. How Do I Manage Information?

In the BRIC, information is power, making it important to reduce the amount of information shared. Details may be removed unless there is a specific need for distribution. Some information may be held back because there is not a need to distribute it. In high-context cultures, data repression is enhanced by assumptions that people already know what needs to be understood.

In the US, information is widely distributed. CEOs share with employees big-picture visions about company goals and why employees are important. Americans have no issue providing details on where things stand with a task, making the quality and quantity of the information distributed high.

Accommodating the two styles is difficult. Make clear what information should be shared at the start of a project. Outline which documents need to be compiled, and put them in a shared location to start this process. With the emergence of virtual tools, such as Wikis, a manager can specifically cite what should be available. This may include information you haven't considered, such as high-level mission statements or how the pieces of the system or process will fit into a larger objective. Be open to having this set of files as a living location where others can add information at will.

Institute an "ask" policy. Make sure your team understands they can always ask for information. The BRIC will likely assume information is not available if they cannot readily find it. An ask policy will make information gathering a BRIC responsibility. This may take time to instill, making it important for you to continually ask, "Do you need more information?"

As an American, be aware that some details may not be flowing back from the BRIC because you have not made yourself a need-to-know participant in the conversation. Work to establish trust and stature inside relationships no matter what your level, and be in the path of information sharing. If it is being shared above your level, engage your boss to be more active in the process.

See also: Managing Communication Technologies

7.3. Managing Decisions

In the US, responsibilities are assigned to individuals who will bring them to fruition. Responsibilities are typically big picture at mid levels of organizations without specific directions on how to accomplish goals. This is called empowered leadership, where employees are empowered to drive objectives in their own manner. Employees are judged on their creative approaches, ability to get resources from the right people in the organization and timely delivery.

In the BRIC, tasks are assigned with specific directions. Subordinates are given specific outlines on how to achieve tasks and must come back to the boss when additional guidance is required. Decisions made outside of the initial directions will be frowned upon. Managers inside the BRIC have specific tasks as well. They are responsible for specific items and actions. When these fall outside of the framework provided, they are deemed as someone else's responsibility and they must ask the manager what to do. At a manager level this is tricky; bringing something that should have already been recognized to their boss's or another manager's attention can cause a loss of face.

This framework creates an environment where constant checking is expected. When running a task-oriented environment, make sure tasks are being accomplished and nothing has fallen into a black hole of unknown responsibilities waiting for approval or for others to figure out approval is needed.

Armed with this knowledge, create the right structures when working with the BRIC. The biggest problem you will encounter is the length of time it takes to get a decision. Remember, all decisions need to be pushed up to the right level where they are discussed with stakeholders. This process will take time, making it important to understand from your contact the process required once a decision is needed.

When managing a project, remember that decisions are only discussed with the relevant stakeholders. Bringing a decision to a conference call, for example, may not be the right forum. You may have a lively conversation with the team about possibilities only to find that the boss needs to make the final call. Think through agenda items that require decisions, and ask who will need to make them.

When a decision is pending, your contact may ignore your attempts to find out more. This person is too low in the hierarchy to know, so instead of talking to you they ignore you, assuming that you will pick up on the high-context hint that you need to go to the manager.

When encountering an "I thought we solved this problem" situation, be aware that the decision was made too low in the hierarchy. What likely happened was that you assumed a decision was made when the group was merely discussing possibilities. Be very clear on decisions. Follow up with written communications to the boss to verify.

See also: Meeting Planning, Planning and Running Conference Calls

I know a professional who spent weeks setting up a meeting in the BRIC about a project that was internal to their organization. Once she arrived in country, her attempts to move forward with the meetings she planned were ignored. The reason? The boss was not party to the conversations and no decision had been made about the meetings.

7.4 Providing Feedback

A client was finishing up a project with a firm in India and she wanted to give feedback but was rejected by the Indian manager. She, as the Project Manger, was accustomed to offering feedback throughout the project lifecycle and had asked many times to do so but was continually rejected. This seemed nonsensical to her but she finally gave up. What she missed was the message the manager was sending to her: she was not important enough to give feedback.

Americans believe providing feedback is essential to improvement. Feedback is not "taken personally" because it's part of the path to improvement. We are taught as managers to notice bad behavior immediately and directly. Providing feedback is possible because we live in a highly individual culture with low power distance. The low power distance makes us think of our boss as more of a peer rather than an elder providing wisdom. For those outside of the boss's wrath who exhibit perfect behavior all year, direct feedback is still forced in the US through yearly employee reviews.

Feedback conflicts with group relationships, high-context communication and hierarchy. Individuals may be called out in the BRIC, but for the most part this is not the case. Avoid individual feedback until you truly understand your BRIC team. Individuals do not work to excel as they do in the US. Instead, contributions are measured as a group. Remember that these are ascription cultures rather than achievement. Excelling is expected rather than used as a route to the fast track of management. Group members earn promotions through time and education, making it clear where everyone stands. Bringing someone into focus inside the group destroys its balance and may greatly embarrass the individual, even causing them to leave the organization.

Feedback should be effective but not direct. Understand how the BRIC manager gives feedback and ask him to include you. The key employee on your project may not get kudos directly, but his team will be highlighted. The idea that behavior needs to be directly acknowledged is part of the American culture. Things such as employee of the month are a great example of loud feedback that is unheard of in these cultures. Finally, providing feedback directly to those lower in the hierarchy will be uncomfortable and will not carry the same weight as if you pass the information up the chain. Use the management hierarchy to make sure the messages are appropriately distributed.

If you are facing problems with feedback, go above the person who has turned you down. By turning down your feedback, a BRIC manager is telling you with high-context messaging that you are not important enough to provide it. This action should immediately put you on notice. Somehow the manager you work with does not see your level of power and importance inside the project. This is a misunderstanding: the manager likely has no idea the weight you hold in the organization. Ask your boss to get involved in this conversation so the voice that you need to express is not lost and so the manager understands the power you have in the organization for future situations.

This rejection of feedback may also be an attempt to avoid handling feedback properly on the management side. If the BRIC manager knows the project is not going well, what better way to hide it from his management by not engaging to receive this information? This is another reason to send a flag up to your manager. Ignoring this rejection is not an option. It sets the stage for future showdowns when big problems present. It's critical as a Desk Diplomat to move to action from cultural understanding. Seeing these problems and taking action will set a new tone inside your project.

In some situations, direct feedback may be an option. Once you arrive at that place, expressing yourself across cultures requires modifications. Indirect communication will be necessary to provide feedback that is heard. Americans are so blunt that instead of hearing us, the BRIC just shuts down. A Brazilian I know says of his American manager, "It sounds like he is going to run me down." Trying giving indirect feedback; it works. For example, tell a story about another project you worked on that was very successful, highlighting what you want to see in this project. Be specific about the behavior that was critical to the success. The hint will come across.

Working across cultures requires doing things that are uncomfortable. The project manager profiled at the start of this section is a good example of avoiding conflict and hoping that things will get better. Don't imagine that eventually the manger will understand your importance. This is not how these cultures work. They understand your rank and responsibility by title, not performance. This is different from the US and is a common mistake. Listen loudly to the messaging being sent to you and be willing to interpret it negatively.

See also: Communicating Effectively, Leading Indirectly

7.5 Leading Indirectly

Indirect leaders face a harrowing task when engaging with the BRIC. If you hold the position of Project Manager, Program Manager or another title given in the US to people who are indirect leaders, you are on the road to one of the most complex tasks Desk Diplomats pursue when working with the BRIC. In the US, indirect leaders are decision makers who manage responsibilities inside flat organization models. They move vague objectives forward using persuasion and high levels of emotional intelligence to get things done. Project Managers understand the heartbeat of organizations and find ways to accomplish things that are way outside their job description.

Indirect leaders often report to more than one person based on a subordinate manager relationship as well as project relationships. They are able to work with multiple superiors because they are assigned responsibilities not tasks; there is no one person telling them specifically how to accomplish goals.

The problem is this is not how the BRIC works. The BRIC relies on one-to-one mapping of manager to subordinate relationships. When individuals hold the titles we associate with indirect leaders, it is likely they are seen as advisors, not leaders. The manager is operating behind the scenes, directing the BRIC project manager in the right direction with specific responsibilities and tasks. When the project manager fails, it's really the manager who fails. If you are aware of this from the start, you will not be surprised by the sudden entry of the manager. It is to your benefit to understand whom that manager is from the start of the project. When you see failure on the horizon, act on it and engage the manager.

Project Managers will be judged by the BRIC as being advisors, not authorities. This is an important distinction because your boss will expect you to negotiate and get decisions that the BRIC may not be willing to provide. If you run into this roadblock, start engaging your boss. Ask her to send a note signaling your authority on the project. After this step, simply copying her on future emails may suffice. Signaling that your boss is involved will unlock problems at the start of a relationship. Over time the other side will begin to see that you are the one driving the project.

One of the problems Project Managers run into is assuming they can corral individuals in the BRIC to join a project team. In the US, project resources are formally and informally assigned. You may need an expert to answer a question in the US. It's unlikely he will go through a formal process to provide an answer beyond noting to his boss that he helped you. This will not work in the BRIC. Full assignment by managers is needed for all project members. Informally asking for help may put team members in a bad position; they will want to please you but they need to work inside their own framework. This may result in your thinking someone on the team is going to help, but he suddenly stops answering emails or phone calls from you.

See also: Giving Feedback, Managing Decisions, Influencing Teams

7.6 Communicating Effectively

The BRIC prefers high-context communication while Americans prefer low-context communication. This difference is enormous when engaging in the initial stages of working together. Americans are naturally direct, so much so that most cultures consider us to be rude and unfeeling. What these cultures are seeing is our ability to have multiple faces inside our lives. Some are personal some are not. These external visitors don't see us in more intimate situations with family members where feelings and other high-context communications are used. If you can see how your personal relationships are different from your work relationships, you are ready to understand how the BRIC communicates. Relationships with parents, siblings, children and spouses are the only exposure we get to high-context communication. Think about the last time you hung up the phone with a family member and thought to yourself, "What were they not telling me"? We often know what these in-group members are trying to say without them having to say it. We finish sentences, see physical cues of distress and interpret use of language at a much higher level.

These are the same skills to take with you when you start interacting with the BRIC. Take these to a conference call, when reviewing emails, looking at Wiki messages and instant messages. Think about the following questions:

- What else might be happening?
- What is not being said?
- Does this person have any involvement or are they a reporter to action?
- Does this communication conflict with previous information?
- Are they answering in a negative or positive way as a default?
- Have I allowed enough time for them to translate messages into English?
- Is this story a way of telling me something important?

For virtual teams, these questions will be harder to answer but they must be asked. Notice excessive communication may be a roundabout way of expressing something that cannot be said. Recognize an email at an odd time may be a message in itself. Understand that ignoring you is not a mistake, it is a message.

It is so important for Americans to understand that things are not said in these cultures, they are understood. Give yourself enough time to review communications and let them sink in before acting on them. Use the above list of questions to get started.

See also: Communication Styles

7.7 Influencing Teams

The BRIC's cultural factors require a different type of leadership. These leaders are close with the group, exchanging responsibility of the group's careers for loyalty. Leaders are more like father figures. Relationships between subordinates and managers feel more like familial American relationships. The distant relationships we have with colleagues literally live in a different world than the close relations expressed by the BRIC. Therefore, when trying to influence remotely, it's critical to appear as a trusted, loyal leader.

Remember that the BRIC is on constant lookout for possible loss of face. Your subordinates will make sure you are behaving in a way that will not cause them to lose face: its part of their identity for you to not embarrass them. Subordinates will also protect you by making sure outsiders are not acting in ways that may cause you to lose face.

As an indirect leader, avoid criticism of managers. Questioning managerial directives is a pathway to losing face and isn't allowed in BRIC cultures. In the US, managers are on a more even plane. We have low power distance and can question objectives and decisions. In high power distance environments this is not possible. Question the manager directly not through the group.

You are the leader, not a follower. This distinction in the BRIC is strong because as a leader you give out directions rather than ask for feedback. Questions such as "How would you do this"? or "What is the best way?" are appropriate for low power distance environments like the US. In the BRIC, individuals become confused, wondering, "If you're the boss, why are you asking me?" Instead, assign the task directly or ask for the group to discuss the pros and cons of two options you propose, and then make the decision for them. This process of open discussion may not be viable in the BRIC organization you are working with so do not get discouraged if no one reacts. Just be clear you will be making the decision after the discussion.

Be open to having closer relationships with your team and the possibility of offering advice. Your team may come to you with personal requests. Each of these will have to be managed separately but understand this is a compliment. The team is seeing you as its leader and someone they admire.

See also: Relationship vs. Venture, The Mystery of Face, Leading Indirectly

7.8 Developing Relationships

Inside the BRIC, business relationships are much more intimate than in the US. Americans have the ability to create multiple identities across different parts of their daily lives and rarely talk about personal matters in a business setting. We may ask, "How are you?" but we rarely want to know the details. We want the colleague or employee to tell us everything is fine. Our ability to have multiple identities frees us from having to offer the same kind of support in business relationships as we do with personal.

While Americans find friendships at work, they rarely emerge with teammates or between boss and employee. Our competitive nature keeps us from aligning closely with those we see jockeying for the same for positions. Relationships often blossom after we leave a company.

In the BRIC, relationships are closer and blurred. Without the ability to create several identities, work identities and life identities overlap. These cultures form in-groups to create a "family" inside the organization. Groups will defend members in the event of a problem; it may never be known who is to blame inside the team. But rest assured the group knows where the problem is and will solve it. Shame is a great pressure point in these groups; it's shameful to do wrong and let down your team. When this shame plays out in the extreme, we see employees quitting or even committing suicide. An employee in China took his life after it was discovered that he lost an iPhone prototype.

While the BRIC is competitive in nature, it also values ascription over achievement, forcing employees to work for the good of the group pushing the corporation forward by supporting those selected to be leaders. It is clear who will ascend the ladder and on what schedule they will ascend based on education and time served. Ascription is something that Americans learn is "bad" in school. It goes against our need to have "the best man win." Ironically, the cultures seeing the most growth in the world in the 21st century use ascription instead of achievement.

When working with the BRIC, relationships must be a focus for the Desk Diplomat. Get ready to talk about items that seem personal. The BRIC is interested in knowing you, and to know someone in a business context means the same thing as knowing him or her in a close friend situation.

Pay attention to dialogue during phone calls, or even take notes so when someone calls you can easily reengage the conversation about more personal topics. You will be asked about children, husbands, wives, parents and other personal topics. Over time conversations will get shorter, but remember they are critical for building relationships.

See also: Women Working in the BRIC

7.9 Recognizing Sincerity

We look for sincerity in many ways during our day. It shows us intention, understanding and trust. Here are some ways we measure sincerity in our culture:

- **Body language**: Appropriate eye contact indicates truth and attentiveness. Posture such as folded arms shows unwillingness.
- **Voice**: Enthusiasm and high energy in a voice enhanced with authority makes Americans believe the person.
- **Smile**: Appropriate smiling or not smiling helps us understand intention.

These are also used in combination with each other. I recently made a trip to the emergency room after slicing my toe open. When the doctor told me what to do after I left the hospital, he was smiling enthusiastically. While I am sure someone taught him to smile as often as possible in the hospital, it came off as inappropriate and fake. We look for things that match: positive information delivered with enthusiasm combined with a smile feels appropriate. Enthusiasm and smiling while delivering somber news seems fake.

Reading sincerity is one of the most important skills of an international businessperson. Our ability to read sincerity is hampered by cultural distance in BRIC relationships. This distance is further magnified when operating as a Desk Diplomat, who works with teams virtually. Communicating via phone and email hampers the ways we establish trust. We must rely on the written word of "I can do it." We think enthusiasm heard over the phone is an indicator. In fact, this should be heard with trepidation. Complexities can be overcome through an understanding of the internal workings of the BRIC as well as being on constant watch for virtual behavior inconsistencies, such as emails indicating agreement not followed by details on how action will take place.

The BRIC focuses on harmony, which means they will do their best to try to please you and the group, even if their words are not sincere. This is critical to understand; harmony has more value than sincerity. In high-context cultures, the expectation is that you will understand the underlying message. Follow your instincts and look at supporting facts. If suddenly it's a yes from India, China and Brazil be aware that this may be an attempt at harmony rather than a real yes. Ask for back-up information on how things will get accomplished. Keep asking for detail on a yes. Know that if your gut is telling you something, you should listen and follow that instinct. Things are a little different in Russia; you may get a no instead of a yes. "No it can't be done," relieves Russians from taking on the task of pushing a new idea forward. It's time to engage the hierarchy and have your boss ask someone higher up to get past an initial no.

One of the ways to check sincerity is to be a micromanager. Including constant check-ins on tasks with milestones will make it clear if the team is in pursuit of its goals as they have obligated themselves to be. As you ask for details on the plan and develop a framework for delivering, it will become clear how flushed out that yes really is.

> A common client problem in this category
> is engaging a vendor to write code in a
> certain language, signing all of the necessary
> contracts with the assertions that the work
> can be done. Months later the code is
> delivered in the wrong language. Contract
> clauses can ensure that the work is redone
> without additional fees, but the project
> will be late. By using micromanagement
> processes, these problems can be avoided

The other sincerity problem is enhanced by power distance. When you ask someone on your team to accomplish and you hear back "yes, it can be done," you may naturally assume all is well because a US colleague would have told you no if he could not accomplish it. The person in the BRIC, however, may say yes assuming you will ask his manager. He will then wait for specific task assignment from his manager. The uninitiated Desk Diplomat will find out a few weeks later when the task was not completed that he missed a step. Make sure you get decisions from decision makers, no matter how small they seem.

See also: Managing Decisions

CHAPTER 8:
TRAVELING TO THE BRIC

When Desk Diplomats do get a chance to travel to meet their teams, they are expected to show up prepared like a well-polished diplomat who has spent time in-country doing business. This section will help you prepare for the visit to the BRIC by discussing what to expect, how to engage and how to present yourself.

Taking the time to prepare for your trip will be critical to its success. The most common mistake Americans make is assuming business in the BRIC will run as smoothly and quickly as the US. The best thing you can do when planning your engagement is giving yourself extra days that allow for informal meetings and schedule mishaps. The preference for relationship building inside the BRIC results in more contact than you would expect inside America. Schedule errors are common and should be expected. When you give yourself extra time everyone wins.

8.1 Using a Translator

> Note: In India, English will be widely used and may be used as a unification language amongst the Indian team who may speak different local languages. A translator is not required in India unless it's clear that the local language will be preferred.

The world speaks English thanks to the British Empire. India uses English as a unification language. China recently committed to training millions to speak English over the next five years, with a goal of pursuing the lucrative service sectors that put India's IT firms on the map. Russians and Brazilians who participate in international relationships will also have English skills, but these may not be as strong as found in India and China. English, however, is the BRIC's second language, which means that these countries will not be able to express themselves as powerfully as they would in their own languages. This is why using a translator is powerful if you have the opportunity.

When starting a project, hire a translator to help you both in person as well as with the preparation of paper documents. Take the time to have all materials translated into the local language (may not be required for India). This is especially important if you are selling products or services to the BRIC. It displays a vested interest in literally speaking their language. Hire more than one translator so you can check interpretations. Many virtual translators are available and might be perfect for reviewing the translated copies from the person you hired to work with in person.

There are many ways to run a strategy with a translator, all of which begin by hiring them before you depart. This allows you to fully brief the translator on your strategy. It also allows you to control the output of the translator. Relying on the partners to translate for you is an invitation to miss out on anything important the BRIC is discussing in their own language. In Russia, the government trains most translators. This is also the case in China, which is not much of a surprise since China is a communist country where organizational leadership is really part of the greater government.

Working across multiple global teams may become complicated if teams prefer to work in their local language. One team I worked with developed a set of key phrases for each language that would alert them to a problem. . Develop a strategy so the translators clearly see problems. When translating across several languages, things are going to be lost. This is not ideal and should be avoided if at all possible.

See also: Meeting Planning

8.2 Using and Finding an Intermediary

Using an intermediary may be the quickest way to get started in the BRIC. Because the BRIC is focused on relationships, involving a known intermediary to help with introductions and vouch for you is a powerful component to starting a relationship. It should be clearly said: Using an intermediary is not a sign of weakness. It is a sign that you understand how to do business in the BRIC.

Selecting an intermediary is complicated but can be done without previous experience. Keep in mind it's critical that you get a good introduction to the intermediary so they can feel good about working with you.
- Put out communications to business partners and friends and ask for contacts that can help you with introductions.
- Search out second and third party connections on social networks and alumni sites.
- Prepare to get intimate with the intermediary. This person needs to be assured that they should vouch for your interests.
- Be clear on the intermediary's relationships with the other side. Does he receive a fee for introductions? Where does he win by participating in the relationship? There are no right or wrong answers to these questions, but you need to know where you stand and where the intermediary stands. Make sure it's a position you can swallow.

Beyond introductions, intermediaries are also used to deliver information and work as advocates. Using them to deliver information happens at executive levels where problems present themselves and are not managed. By asking a trusted third party to step into the relationship, the partner is forced to listen. Selecting an intermediary to deliver information should be done carefully.

See also: Women Working in the BRIC

8.3 Selecting a Representative to Send to the BRIC

Many organizations make bad choices on whom to send where and why. The first item to consider before selecting someone is his title. Are you willing to borrow a more powerful title for this person so he can accomplish the mission? In the BRIC, hierarchy rules. Therefore, it is critical to show up with powerful people who show the significance of the deal to your corporation. I am not encouraging you to send someone based solely on their title, but consider titles, they will be important. Sending a program manger to do a vice president's job is a lose/lose situation. The BRIC counterpart will quickly be convinced of your lack of seriousness.

The next factor is experience. Does this person possess a passport? Have they worked internationally before? Do they work virtually with international counterparts? I provide my clients with assessment tools to determine who in the organization is the most internationally competent right now and who will be the easiest to train. Using assessment tools before an international assignment is powerful to make sure your own confidence is instilled in the selection as well as ensuring the longevity of the selected employee.

Which brings me to the next factor: Don't send someone with one foot out the door to the BRIC. This guarantees that the time the person spends developing a relationship will be useless the day they depart your organization. The BRIC is focused on building relationships, making it imperative that you send someone who will engage counterparts and build long-term relationships. Ask yourself, "Am I prepared to be engaged in this employee's success and long-term career ambitions?" If the answer is no, don't send this person. Any one-time win without a relationship will be short lived and based on a belief system that the BRIC does not value.

Select at least two people to lead a mission to the BRIC: one with the internationally savvy to communicate in country and one with the strategic background to put a plan in place. The communicator can lead meetings while the strategic can leverage translators, intermediaries and build the right message for the partner behind the scenes.

Building a solid picture of the organization is your goal before you depart. Leverage an intermediary if this is the first time you are working in a country and don't have references. If you are in a competitive situation, it will be critical to commit more time than usual to wining and dining executives, getting to know them well and giving them a chance to sniff you out.

Put a plan in place for transitioning those involved in developing the initial relationship to those who will run the project. The leads who developed the relationship must stay involved but not to the determinant of letting the managers lead the project.

See also: Using and Finding an Intermediary, Using Translators, Meeting Planning

8.4. Women Working in the BRIC

Women have a tougher time working with the BRIC because these cultures are more masculine than the US. When a culture is masculine, it believes strongly in roles for women and men. This means you need to be on a higher guard to defend your position in the group. Constantly asserting yourself with your business card and credentials is required. The BRIC will automatically assume you are the assistant, lover or professional coffee fetcher. It took me 30 minutes to figure out this had happened to me once during a business meeting inside the BRIC. Everyone was engaging the male on my team and ignoring me.

In my experience, this cultural difference is further enhanced by unexpected questions about personal lives. Questions that most women believe are part of their non-work identity are asked by total strangers in the BRIC. "Do you have children?" "Are you married?" "Why or why not?" These are not an off-limits. In the BRIC, the focus will be on you and who you are, not your company. Figure out how you are going to answer these questions in societies that are focused on family. Develop something that is honest, but that also avoids loss of face. Saying something like "I have no interest in children" will not go over well. "I have not yet had the chance to have children" is better.

If you are a mother, these cultures will not resent that you are not with your children. Business circles are composed of mostly higher classes that employ nannies or other caretakers in their lives. Simply say that your children are in the care of their nanny or family at home. End of story.

Be open to seeing that someone may resist doing business with you because of your female status. I suggest not forcing this and inviting an intermediary to the table. We come from a culture that believes that women and men are equal. This belief may not work in situations outside of the US, especially in places like the BRIC. Taking on an intermediary is not a failure; it is a mediation to get the job done. It's more professional to recognize the problem instead of trying to bully your way through it.

Women need to take every level of engagement seriously when it comes to working across cultures. Before you engage in a meeting with the BRIC, take time to research with whom you will be meeting, where their views were built and how this may impact you. The closer we are to another's experiences the more we are able to understand it.

- It's helpful to understand if those you are engaging with are old or young. Working with younger businessmen will be easier than older men who have had years of training to keep women out of the picture and little experience dealing with us.
- Look to see if any of your counterparts have trained outside of their home country at prestigious schools. This experience will have put them inside different cultures where women were involved on a business level.

- Understand where else they have worked. This information can be found on company websites, alumni sites or on social networking locations like LinkedIn.
- Try to piece together what counterparts' lives look like and how this lens affects their view of you. Are they married to someone with a career or someone who stays home? They may be supportive of you if they support that same idea at home. Do they have a daughter who is successful and perhaps breaking the mold of women's role expectations in country? They may support you internally because of their support of their daughter.
- Think of items they will want to talk about based on what you have found. Try to find similar interests or topics that you can speak informatively about. These subtleties are expected of women and will be well received.

See also: The Mystery of Face, Dinner Meetings, Dressing for Success

8.5 Dinner Meetings

When meeting live with BRIC counterparts, it's important to think about hierarchy in social situations. The boss or leader of the organization will be sitting at either the head or the middle of the table. As introductions are made before dinner, take note of business cards or verbal titles that are passed in conversations. Be conscientious that the expectation will be to match your contingent with the BRIC group at the table by title. Sitting next to the boss is a must for the leader of your organization as well as trying to match similar skill sets for the rest of the group.

Dinner may occur at a restaurant or at the boss's home. No matter where, the boss will set the tone for the evening. He will instruct on when to eat, what to eat, how to eat and if drinking is appropriate. He will decide if it's appropriate to include spouses. If you are uncertain about protocols, ask if you should be prepared to meet his wife this evening, or if that will happen at another time. This gives the boss an out to offer another time to meet his wife.

Before going to dinner, make sure you understand a bit about the food of the BRIC cultures. I advise my clients to have a list of things they know they like if they have the opportunity to order. It's important to make the right accommodations for you and your host. In Brazil more meats will be served than in India. Think about this in both directions: if you are a vegetarian, read up on your options so you do not offend. If you are not a vegetarian, watch what others order and follow suit so you do not offend. If everyone is eating vegetarian, it won't hurt you to go meatless for the evening.

Most cultures are excited to share their food; it is a way they express themselves. Try to have a few dinners in local restaurants if possible while traveling through these countries. It will give you something to discuss when you meet for business dealings, and it will make the BRIC feel you are interested in the relationship. It's funny how food leads to feelings of love and appreciation inside a marriage as well as international business relationships.

8.6 Dressing for Success

The American workplace has become so lax in our use of formal dress that many people feel that dressing up is no longer a requirement. This could not be further from the truth when working across cultures. Across the BRIC, formal and informal dress is used to show roles. In these cultures, hierarchy and power distance force the adoption of appropriate dress to help identify a person's importance.

A friend recently landed in Russia in sweat pants and was annoyed that everyone was glaring at her and treating her badly. "Everyone had a mink coat on and high heels," she said. Of course they did! This is how they display their membership to a higher class of people through prominent display of fancy clothing, luggage and shoes.

Avoid wearing khakis and a golf shirt, which shows disrespect to the importance of a meeting and to you. Opt for a suit at all times. If you check your luggage, wear a formal shirt on the plane so you are prepared when you arrive. It's extremely difficult in the BRIC to get the right wardrobe pieces that fit an American frame within a short time. You may not need to wear a tie, but always wear a suit. You may want to start with a tie and see how it goes. This outfit will display one thing: I am important and I take myself seriously.

For women, the advice is the same. Wear a suit. If you want to wear a skirt, please make sure it hits your knees. Bring hose; it will be worn unless it's hot. Dress conservatively unless this is not part of your brand. Be true to who you are in a way that conveys your message without seeming too sexual. Invest in something that makes you appear to be the professional that you are.

Women have an additional challenge when they travel to the BRIC; these countries still have strong ideas that men run the world and women stay at home watching the family. They will do business with you, but they will wish you were a male. This means you must look great, managing a professional appearance at all times.

See also: Women Working with the BRIC

> *A woman who wanted to wear Chico's outfits while in China recently approached me. "They are so easy to pack," she said. From my own personal experience I can assure you that good quality wools are easy to pack and, if wrapped in dry cleaning bags, come out in great shape. I have trucked my favorite wool dresses around the world several times and they continue to look fantastic. Take yourself seriously by dressing for success rather than a casual interaction.*

Chapter 9: Closing Words

American organizations have not focused on building global competencies in the past because our organizational model has been extremely successful. While our model continues to bring success, our reliance on external partnerships will grow rapidly over the next decade. The chances of an organization engaging a partner in the BRIC increase every day.

Executives are frustrated by the complexity of this new environment citing cultural differences as one of their biggest obstacles to success. When not properly managed, multi-cultural project teams have astronomical turnover rates, are highly inefficient, fail to deliver in a timely fashion, and fail to perform in the same way as a home-based mono-cultural teams. Organizational leaders want to take advantage of global opportunities from a balance sheet perspective, but those in middle management encounter great difficulty delivering the financial promise their superiors demand.

Today we focus on those sent overseas to establish and manage relationships by providing them with the same cultural training diplomats receive. Organizations need to consider those left behind, the Desk Diplomats who work with international counterparts on a daily basis from their desk, rarely getting to travel. These workers are the action underlying all multi-national projects.

The main problem with cross-cultural training is that it's only informative. There is no action. Students walk away with information but are unsure how to leverage it inside daily actions. Organizations need to offer employees a way to become globally competent.

The four global competencies my practice instills are as follows:
- Intercultural Awareness
- Intercultural Communication
- Building Commitment
- Managing Uncertainty

These four factors start with education on partner cultures to generate awareness, but with awareness comes the ability to communicate and to move forward with teams that need commitment to be successful. These teams also need leaders to manage the uncertainty of working across cultures. This four-point model engages both the employee and the employer. These competencies can be added to review processes just like general competencies expected inside every job profile. By making cultural competence part of job responsibilities organizations demand action.

There is a perception that some of us are naturally cross-culturally competent. This is not true. It is impossible for us to understand how a culture is different from ours inside a remote business relationship. Often organizations assume the strong skills that create committed teams we see at home can easily be leveraged inside different cultures. While highly valued here, these skills fail inside the BRIC. These cultures believe things are true that we believe are false. By not offering a roadmap to these differences, Americans become frustrated and projects are delayed or fail. These stories can be avoided when organizations take steps to educate and train workers to become Desk Diplomats.

CHAPTER 10:
BUSINESS CULTURE
PREFERENCES QUIZ

This short quiz will give you insight into your own preferences. Select 1 if the statement aligns with your experience. If the statement is far from your experience, select 5.

SECTION 1: *Communication Style*

Telling stories about a "friend" in difficulty is a good way to explain to my boss what the problem is.

1 2 3 4 5

Saying yes, when it can't be done, is the best way. The boss knows it can't be done without me telling him.

1 2 3 4 5

TOTAL _____

SECTION 2: Organizational Structure

At work, decisions are made by the boss and are handed down without questions to subordinates. Subordinates must follow directives.

1 2 3 4 5

At work, titles such as Mr. or Mrs. are used to address senior members of the organization.

1 2 3 4 5

TOTAL _____

SECTION 3: *Power Distance*

At work, it's ok to offer feedback
to my boss on how he is doing.

1 2 3 4 5

At work, it is often hard to tell
who is managing and who is being
managed.

1 2 3 4 5

TOTAL  _____

SECTION 4: Individual vs. Group

Inside a family, children are taught that their opinion matters and should be heard.

1 2 3 4 5

Once people graduate they are expected to move out and live on their own.

1 2 3 4 5

TOTAL _____

SECTION 5: Relationship vs. Venture

At work we do business with the firm that has the best product irrespective of the group selling the product.

1 2 3 4 5

At work I avoid doing business with people I know well to avoid a conflict of interest.

1 2 3 4 5

TOTAL _____

Total your scores for each section and write in how you compare to US and BRIC preferences.

	Your Score
Total for Section 1 How Organizations Communicate	
Total for Section 2 How Decisions are Managed	
Total for Section 3 How Power Is Distributed	
Total for Section 4 How Employees Work Together	
Total for Section 5 How Organizations Engage Partners	

US preferences score closer to:	BRIC Preferences score closer to:
10	2
10	2
2	10
2	10
2	10

Chapter 11: Resources

Books

Extreme Project Management by Doug DeCarlo

This book offers a comprehensive method for fast moving projects. This is method can easily be applied to global projects and will benefit managers trying to establish a more micro-managed approached to projects as I recommend in this book.

Negotiating Globally: How to Negotiate Deals, Resolve Disputes and Make Decisions Across Cultural Boundaries by Jeanne M. Brett

This book will serve as a guide to any cross-cultural manager who negotiates with teams daily to get projects completed. Brett included a section on working with governments and social issues. She also focuses on negotiation strategy when working with partners that don't think win/loose at the negotiation table.

Making Things Happen: Mastering Project Management by Scott Berkun

Berkun does not speak about international differences in this book but it's a solid example of a project management structure that will work with global teams. Good for problem solving.

Riding the Waves of Culture by Fons Trompenaars and Charles Hampden-Turner

Trompenaars, a student of Hofstede, offers an in-depth look at how business cultures unfold and effect results. This book is academic and practical at the same time and a must read for those engaging with multiple cultures.

Influencer: The Power to Change Anything
by Kerry Patterson, Joseph Grenny, David Maxfield, Ron McMillan and Al Switzler

Written by the same team as Crucial Conversations this book offers insight into problem solving by guiding you through situations and revealing unique solutions. This book is a must read for any global manager. It teaches you how to think openly about situations you don't understand.

The Culture Code by Clotaire Rapaille

This is a book about America from the inside out and the outside in. Rapaille develops codes, or one-word descriptions, for things and explains why. Offers much insight into how Americans see themselves and aspects of their culture. Also tells some harsh truths of how the world sees Americans.

When Cultures Collide: Leading Across Cultures
by Richard D. Lewis

Covering 60 countries this book is a reference guide for the global manager. Lewis uses his own method for describing the cultures, which can be confusing, but if you ignore his attempt to classify every country as linear, multi or reactive the data provided on each country is well researched and detailed. This book offers the ability to have one desk reference at the ready.

The Dance of Life by Edward T. Hall

Hall was the first to suggest many things about cultures and this book reads like an esoteric old classic that you pick up occasionally. Hall came to the US from Germany during World War II and spent his life studying cultural differences between Americans, Germans and the rest of the world.

The Project Management Tool Kit: 100 Tips and Techniques for Getting the Job Done Right
by Tom Kendrick

Step by step this book takes you through 100 possible situations with solutions. It can easily be used across cultures once you understand what American preferences will be and how to contrast them with those of your partner. I like this book because it identifies many problems with solutions that an international project manager may not recognize until it's too late. I suggest reviewing the back section of this book before starting an international project.

International Project Management by Bennet P. Leintz and Kathryn P. Rea

Project management solutions for international projects. It outlines several problems that should be on your radar when getting started.

Crucial Conversations: Tools for Talking when Stakes are High
by Kerry Patterson, Joseph Grenny, Ron McMillan and Al Switzler

The tools in this book are designed to trigger responses in your brain in the middle of difficult conversations. One of the biggest challenges as a global manager is doing things that feel uncomfortable. Crucial Conversations is all about how to manage action consciously and unconsciously when in stressful conversations.

How We Compete: What Companies Around the World are Doing to Make it in Today's Global Economy
by Suzanne Berger

The findings of the MIT study of 500 international companies are outlined in this book. This book provides detailed insight into how Asian countries have taken bold steps to secure offshore markets.

Cultures and Organizations: Software for the Mind
by Geert Hofstede

Hofstede spent his life studying IBM and other global corporations trying to decode the differences displayed across different countries. This is his most concise work written in straightforward Dutch style.

Six Thinking Hats
by Edward De Bono

It's useful to bring formal problem solving methods to the table when working with international teams on a shared issue. Using the thinking hats presented by De Bono in this book is one way to conquer complexity and bring out insights held across teams.

The Lexus and the Olive Tree
by Thomas Friedman

This is Friedman's first look at globalization. He was one of the first thinkers to identify how globalization was arriving in today's technological environment.

Managing People Across Cultures
by Fons Trompenaars

Tropenaars has some strong points in this book that are worth a reading if you are integrating two cultures after a merger or heavily relying on your captive center to generate innovation. The text is for the advanced global manager.

Imaging India: The Idea of a Renewed Nation
by Nandan Nilekani
Nilekani is one of the founders of Infosys and a provoking thought leader. This book offers a historical and forward look at where India came from, where she stands today and where the opportunity lies for the future. A must read for those managing Indian teams.

A Gift to My Children: A Father's Lessons for Life and Investing
by Jim Rogers
Rogers is a money manager, a very wealthy one at that. He spent a year traveling the globe in a specialized Mercedes across African deserts, rainforests in the Amazon and all of Asia. This trip made him see how the world is changing causing him to move his young children to Asia to integrate them into where he sees the world's power shifting. This book is a short work with insights both personal and worldly on what global trends mean in today's environment.

The Fortune at the Bottom of the Pyramid
by C. K. Prahalad
The number of people living in the BRIC that are in poverty creates a large market for retailers that figure out how to tap the market. This book walks through Prahalad's thoughts on how to eradicate poverty and consider these millions as a possible market.

Reading People: How to Understand People and Predict Their Behavior Anytime, Anyplace
by Jo-Ellan Dimitrius and Mark Mazzarella
This book teaches how to receive indirect messages based on Dimitrius's experiences as a jury consultant. It's useful to managers working across the BRIC who need to hone indirect skills.

Billions: Selling to the New Chinese Consumer
by Tom Doctoroff

What do the Chinese want? This book speaks to the question by talking about how the Chinese are different from Americans. While this book focuses on the opportunity of the Beijing Olympics of 2008 it remains a primer past its due date.

China Vignettes: An Inside Look at China
by Dominic Barton

Barton leads the McKinsey practice inside Asia and tells compelling, personal stories of the Chinese in this book. It has interviews with hundreds of Chinese that speak to the complexity of China's changes and how they are impacting the population.

When a Billion Chinese Jump: How China will Save Mankind or Destroy It
by Jonathan Watts

I recently heard Watts speak about his book, which is an eco-travelogue by his own account. Watts talks about China's issues and attempts at solutions including water losses, damage to populations through pollution, and attempts to shift to green energy.

Works That Work
by Dr. Frank Lutz

The American culture is focused on word choice. Lutz is the master of phrases that propagate through our culture such as "The Death Tax" instead of the "Estate Tax." This book offers insight into how Americans take in words and how minor shifts impact interpretations and actions.

Online Resources

The Financial Times: Beyond BRICS
Located at **http://blogs.ft.com/beyond-brics/**

FT's newest section is updated daily with articles about the BRIC and other strong emerging markets.

Goldman Sachs Ideas: BRICs
Located at **http://www2.goldmansachs.com/ideas/brics/index.html**

Goldman Sachs updates this site frequently adding video and quarterly reporting on the BRIC

YouTube.com
Searching YouTube for Jim O'Neil, the economist who first developed the BRIC acronym offers a plethora of interviews on the BRIC. Jim O'Neil has spoken about the BRIC all over the world making these videos very insightful.

McKinsey Quarterly
Located at **https://www.mckinseyquarterly.com/**

I suggest getting on McKinsey's free mailing list. The research McKinsey gives away for free is extremely valuable to the global manager.

The Global Manager
Located at **http://theglobalmanager.com**

The Global Manager Program is a two-day intensive given four times a year to develop an elite group of global managers. This site has more information on the program and a host of resources for the international manager.

Are You Ready for the Next Level?

One way to learn more about global competencies is to purchase a personalized Cultural Competency Profile. This profile will become a framework for you to leverage as you engage across business cultures.

In an exciting development these profiles, previously only available in live consulting sessions, are now available online. The Cultural Competency Profile leverages the AIM process:

Assess
Existing cross-cultural capabilities
Existing cultural preferences

Identify
Evaluation of a partner business culture

Mediate
Personalized mediation strategies

When the Cultural Competency Profile is completed you will have a personalized action plan that consists of the following information:

- *Understanding of your cultural preferences & those of your business partner.*
- *Personalized strategies for you to employ to grow global competence*
- *Personalized mediation strategies to use with international partner*

To learn more about the AIM Cultural Competency Profile go to
http://TheGlobalManager.com/CultureCompetencyProfile.
Enter coupon code **BRICBK** *to receive a* **$40 discount** *on the profile.*

Made in the USA
Charleston, SC
05 August 2013